LET'S RELATE TO
GENETICS

Plant Cells

Penny Dowdy

Crabtree Publishing Company

www.crabtreebooks.com

Crabtree Publishing Company

www.crabtreebooks.com

Author: Penny Dowdy
Coordinating editor: Chester Fisher
Series editor: Jessica Cohn
Editorial director: Kathy Middleton
Editor: Adrianna Morganelli
Proofreader: Reagan Miller
Production coordinator: Katherine Berti
Prepress technician: Katherine Berti
Project manager: Kumar Kunal (Q2AMEDIA)
Art direction: Harleen Mehta (Q2AMEDIA)
Cover design: Tarang Saggar (Q2AMEDIA)
Design: Neha Kaul and Tarang Saggar (Q2AMEDIA)
Photo research: Mariea Janet (Q2AMEDIA)

Cover:

Main image:
The Carefree Spirit rose is a hybrid plant bred for better disease resistance.

Inset image:
A microscopic view of the leaf surface of a spiderwort plant shows the stomata, or pores, in the leaf.

Are a plant's cells more complex than yours?:
Yes, they are more complex. Plants have more kinds of cell structures than animals do. They produce their own foods, withstand forces from nature without protective coatings, and survive without shelter.

Photographs:

123RF: Steeve Roche: p. 8-9; N.A. Planken-Kooij: p. 11 (bottom left)
Alamy: Nigel Cattlin: p. 24
All-America Rose Selection: cover
American Honda Motor Co., Inc.: p. 11 (top right)
BigStockPhoto: Georgios Alexandris: p. 31 (top); Jens Herrndorff: p. 35
Corbis: Bettmann: p. 13; Lester V. Bergman: p. 14-15; Carlos Cazalis: p. 41 (top); Wendy Stone: p. 43
Dreamstime: Qyshanghai: p. 4; Rainer Junker: p. 6 (center); Lisey Kina: p. 33
Fotolia: Garry Delong: p. 21 (right); James Martz: p. 27
Istockphoto: Ian Hubball: p. 1, p. 25; Ewen Cameron: p. 6 (top); Joan Wynn: p. 6 (bottom); Phil Sigin: p. 7 (top right); Alexandra Draghici: p. 8 (bottom left); AndreasReh: p. 14 (bottom right); Stuart Duncan Smith: p. 17 (bottom); Armin Hornung: p. 19 (right); Craig Wactor: p. 23; Stanley Lange: p. 40
NOAA Photo Library: p. 42
Photolibrary: Nils-Johan Norenlind: p. 5 (top); R&R Fotos: p. 16 (background); Botanica: p. 29; David Cavagnaro: p. 31 (bottom); Lynne Brotchie: p. 32; Mark Turner: p. 39
Rex Features: p. 37
Shutterstock: Jubal Harshaw: cover; Sasha Buzko: p. 5 (bottom); Westlaker: p. 7 (bottom left); Shutterstock: p. 8 (bottom left), p. 20; Green Stock Creative: p. 8 (bottom left); Rafa Irusta: p. 10; Bestweb: p. 12; Pakhnyushcha: p. 16; Jubal Harshaw: p. 17 (top); Jubal Harshaw: p. 18 (center), p. 19 (left); Ismael Montero Verdu: p. 18 (bottom); Beata Becla: p. 18-19; Mopic: p. 21 (left); Norman Chan: p. 26; Robert Redelowski: p. 34 (center); Mau Horng: p. 34 (bottom); David Koscheck: p. 36-37; Elder Vieira Salles: p. 38; Jeanne Hatch: p. 41 (bottom); Yuri Shirokov: p. 44
Q2AMedia Art Bank: p. 13, 22-23, 28, 30, 33, 45

Library and Archives Canada Cataloguing in Publication

Dowdy, Penny
    Plant cells / Penny Dowdy.

(Let's relate to genetics)
Includes index.
ISBN 978-0-7787-4946-2 (bound).--ISBN 978-0-7787-4963-9 (pbk.)

    1. Plant cells and tissues--Juvenile literature. I. Title. II. Series: Let's relate to genetics

QK725.D69 2009   j571.6'2   C2009-903980-X

Library of Congress Cataloging-in-Publication Data

Dowdy, Penny.
    Plant cells / Penny Dowdy.
        p. cm. -- (Let's relate to genetics plant cells)
    Includes index.
    ISBN 978-0-7787-4963-9 (pbk. : alk. paper) -- ISBN 978-0-7787-4946-2 (reinforced library binding : alk. paper)
    1. Plant cells and tissues--Juvenile literature. I. Title. II. Series.

QK725.D68 2010
580--dc22
                                    2009025289

Crabtree Publishing Company

www.crabtreebooks.com   1-800-387-7650

Printed in the U.S.A./112011/IB20111025

Published in Canada
Crabtree Publishing
616 Welland Ave.
St. Catharines, ON
L2M 5V6

Published in the United States
Crabtree Publishing
PMB 59051
350 Fifth Avenue, 59th Floor
New York, New York 10118

Published in the United Kingdom
Crabtree Publishing
Maritime House
Basin Road North, Hove
BN41 1WR

Published in Australia
Crabtree Publishing
386 Mt. Alexander Rd.
Ascot Vale (Melbourne)
VIC 3032

Contents

Chapter 1

Tiny Treasure

Corn and soybeans can become fuel to replace gasoline. The flowers and leaves of rainforest plants can cure deadly diseases. Many plants have value to humans everywhere. Yet what good is a weed?

Duckweed is invasive, yet it can also make dirty water clean enough to drink.

The plants we do not value are considered weeds. Yet even weeds can have hidden gifts. Duckweed was named because it is a weed and a nuisance in duck ponds. Duckweed is the world's smallest flowering plant. It grows in still waters. The plant has no more than a few leaves, each smaller than your fingernail. One small root dangles from each leaf. Each leaf can break off and start a new plant, which grows quickly. A cluster of duckweed can double within two days.

A Water Filter

Recently, scientists have discovered that this tiny aquatic plant is a natural water filter. It can change sewage into safe drinking water. What is duckweed to some may be a miracle to others.

Standing Tall

A plant, not an animal, is the largest living organism in the world. The California redwood can grow for thousands of years, reaching heights of over 350 feet (107 m). Some of the largest redwoods are over 20 feet (six m) across, and still growing! A plant is also the oldest living organism. Bristlecone pines have grown in California for over 4,000 years.

Plants provide food, clothing, medicine, and even oxygen.

Duckweed, like all plants, is made of plant **cells**. Plant cells do amazing work. They take in sunlight. Plant cells make oxygen that animals need to survive. Plant cells form the basis of all life on Earth.

bristlecone pine

Chapter 2

Seeds of Science

Have you ever wondered which plants near your home are poisonous, and which you can eat? Ancient people asked these same questions.

Long before we knew about cells, the early study of plants led people to discover plants with healing properties. Over 10,000 years ago, people began growing crops they could eat. Through trial and error, they knew which plants to grow. They placed plants into simple groups. For example, a plant was wild or tame, or it was good for food or medicine.

Cacao, from the Americas, is the basic ingredient in chocolate.

Some cultures believed that plants could think and have feelings. Around 400 B.C., the Greeks took a scientific approach. They studied plants, water, and soil to improve their crops. This was the start of the science of **botany**. *Botany* comes from the Greek word *botanikos*, which means "plant." The Greeks put plants into groups, such as trees, shrubs, and herbs. The Greeks also studied how plants grew, reproduced, and died.

Some cultures continued to believe that plants had strange powers. A chain of daisies around a child's neck warded off fairies. Dried ferns protected people from lightning. Holly kept others safe from witchcraft. Science proved these beliefs false. Yet this folklore continued for centuries.

Land Explorations

When explorers from European nations went to new lands, they brought home new plants. Peanuts from South America came to Spain, and then Africa. Explorers brought cacao beans, chili peppers, and potatoes back from the Americas in the sixteenth century. The knowledge of new plant species expanded rapidly as cultures encountered one another.

Chili peppers are used for food and medicines.

Wisdom from the Ancients
Theophrastus
(372 B.C. – 287 B.C.) was an ancient Greek philosopher. He wrote scientific works on botany. *A History of Plants* discusses the parts of plants and the differences between wild and tame plants. *About the Reasons of Vegetable Growth* studies growth, diseases, and taste. People studied his ideas for over a thousand years.

An Onion by Any Other Name

Imagine being sent on a search for the bog onion. As you ask different people, they show you an Indian turnip, a brown dragon, a cuckoo plant, a memory root, and a devil's ear. Yet they all show you the same plant!

Linnaeus Steps In

Plants are called different things in different parts of the United States and in different parts of the world. Several hundred years ago, people published plant information in whatever language they spoke. A French scientist would use a French word to name a plant. A Spanish scientist would use Spanish. This naming method was often confusing.

In the eighteenth century, the Swedish botanist Carolus Linnaeus tried to end this confusion. He created a **binomial nomenclature** system. *Binomial* means "two names." *Nomenclature* comes from a Greek word meaning "name." For example, the bog onion now has the two-word name *Arisaema triphyllum*.

Now, nearly all living things are classified into main groups and subgroups. The main group is made up of a **genus**, and contains a huge number of living things. The genus *Arisaema*, for example, includes flowering plants that grow from bulbs. The subgroups are classified by different **species**.

All the cultivars listed are red maples. *Acer* is the genus for "maple," and *rubrum* is the species name for "red."

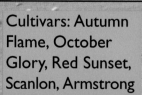

Cultivars: Autumn Flame, October Glory, Red Sunset, Scanlon, Armstrong

The bog onion is part of the species triphyllum. Some species are also broken into **cultivars**, or special varieties. Botanists know of at least three cultivars of *Arisaema triphyllum*.

With this system, scientists could finally understand each other. If a British researcher wrote about the *Ocimum basilicum*, a French botanist would know he or she is writing about basil.

Oh, Snap!
Linnaeus named plants for people. If he liked or respected people, he named a beautiful or well-regarded plant after them. The magnolia tree has fragrant blossoms. He named that for a friend. Linnaeus named a tiny weed that grows only in mud after one of his critics.

Until the eighteenth century, any plant in any landscape had any number of names.

9

Hybrids Are Not Just Cars

Have you ever seen a purple, red, or yellow carrot? Centuries ago, people found different types of carrots in many places. Then the Dutch created a **hybrid** carrot that was orange. The orange carrots became popular throughout the world.

Choosing a Plant's Traits

Plants have undergone **selective breeding** for thousands of years. During the Stone Age, people picked seeds from wild grasses and planted the seeds of plants they liked best. They noticed which plants were best at resisting diseases. Early farmers paid attention to which plants were more nutritious. Over many generations, these plants developed into corn, wheat, and rice.

In the eighteenth century and beyond, people started looking at other ways to improve crops. Researchers studied plant breeding. For example, they would cross a corn plant that produced many ears with a corn plant that resisted diseases. The offspring had some traits of both parents. After a few plant generations, the farmers had a corn hybrid that was better than the original. Sometimes, these experiments took many years before farmers reached the right result.

Dutch scientists created an orange carrot hybrid to match the color of their national flag.

Sometimes people created hybrids because of the plants' beauty. For example, gardeners could grow roses and tulips with specific colors or number of petals.

These colorful summer phlox are just one of numerous hybrid versions.

Breeding New Concepts

Before the nineteenth century, people rarely used the word *hybrid*. It comes from a Latin word meaning "mongrel." Originally, a mongrel was the offspring of a wild boar and tame pig. The offspring was a new species, different from either parent. Botanists adopted the concept. Now, the car industry has adopted the word *hybrid*. For a century, most cars ran on gasoline. The popular hybrid cars of today have engines that can run on gas and electricity. These cars use two different fuels.

What Plants Inherit

Botanists and backyard gardeners have long made hybrids by crossing plants. They did this for so long before they understood the science behind their actions. Until Gregor Mendel explained inheritance, creating a plant with a desired trait was an unreliable process.

Mendel's Alleles

In the 1800s, Mendel formed ideas about inheritance in plants and animals. Mendel used garden pea plants to test his ideas. He developed three theories.

- A male or female sex cell has an **allele** for each trait. In the pea plant, for example, each parent has an allele for flower color. The two alleles combine in a new plant. The combined alleles give the offspring the directions for the color of its flowers.
- Every set of alleles ends up giving instructions for one trait. There is a pair of alleles for flower color, for example, with one allele from the mother and one from the father. The alleles for color do not control other characteristics.
- Alleles can be **dominant** or **recessive**. A dominant trait wins out. The trait for purple flowers is dominant, so a plant will produce purple flowers if just one of its alleles carries instructions for purple. The trait for white flowers is recessive. That means an offspring would need the white allele from both parents in order to have white flowers.

The common garden pea plant helped Gregor Mendel develop his ideas about inherited traits.

Punnett Squares Showing Purple and White Pea Flowers

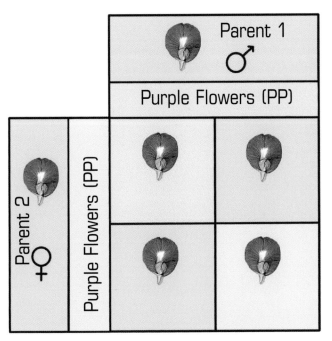

In this diagram, both purple parents have two purple alleles. The two parent plants will produce purple offspring.

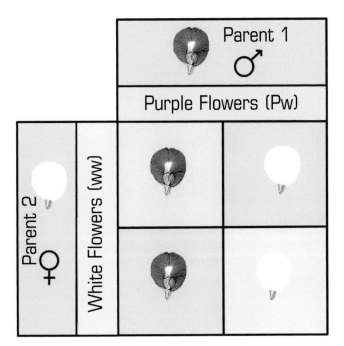

In this diagram, the purple flower has one purple allele and one white allele. When the purple and white flowers combine, the offspring could be purple or white.

Near Miss

Gregor Mendel did his research on inheritance in pea plants in the mid 1800s. However, his ideas were not widely accepted until the 1900s. At that point, botanists rediscovered his work. He did not live to get recognition for his important discoveries. Today Mendel is known as the Father of Genetics.

Ready for a Close-Up

Scientists experimented with plants for hundreds of years. Scientists did not understand what happened inside a plant. They could only make educated guesses. They could see evidence of changes in a plant. Yet until microscopes were available, scientists did not know for certain how the changes happened.

Hooked on Plants

Robert Hooke was, by all accounts, an amazing scientist. He dabbled in chemistry, physics, astronomy, geology, biology, and architecture. He was friends with Isaac Newton. He invented dozens of important machines. Hooke excelled in every area of science that he worked in.

Hooke built a microscope that allowed him to look at small things and study them closely. He examined bird feathers, sponges, insects, and more. In 1665, he described his findings in a book called *Micrographia*.

In that book, Hooke describes the small slice of cork that he viewed in the microscope. He describes what he saw as being like a honeycomb, but with shapes that were not all the same. He called these shapes cells. This was a huge discovery. At the time, however, Hooke did not understand how important cells were.

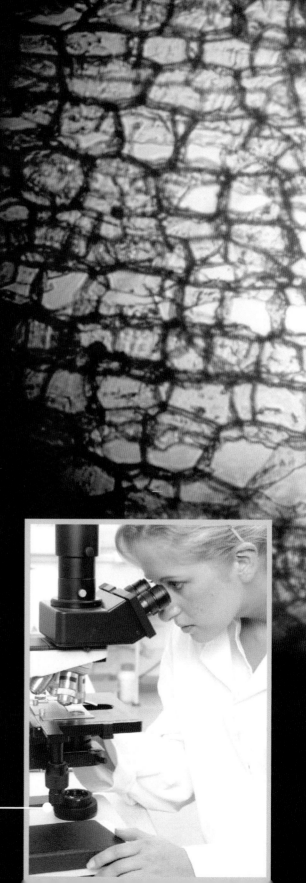

The microscope has advanced the study of plant cells and genetics.

14

Going by What You Know
Hooke described the shapes
he saw on the cork slide as
cells. Their rectangular shape
looked like walls. He had lived
in a monastery, where the
rooms were called cells,
so he named the shapes
for the rooms.

Cork cells, magnified 100
times, look like a honeycomb.

Schleiden and Schwann

Over 100 years later, Matthias Schleiden studied plant cells
under a microscope. No matter what part of the plant he
looked at, he saw cells. Another scientist, Theodor Schwann,
found the same thing with animal cells. The two men shared
their findings and determined that all living things must be
made of cells. Schwann published their findings in 1838 but
gave no credit to Schleiden.

Chapter 3

Plant Cell Science

As Schleiden and Schwann discovered, plant and animal cells are alike in many ways. All plant tissue is made of cells. All animal tissue is made of cells, too. Cells are the building blocks of all living things.

Plants and animals have similar cell structure. They are both **eukaryotes**. Eukaryotes are living things made of one or more cell. Every cell of eukaryotes has a **nucleus** and other **organelles**.

Though plant and animal cells are certainly different, they have similar organelles. First, they both have **plasma membranes**. The membrane controls what comes in and out of the cell. This protects the cell from harmful materials. It allows helpful substances such as nutrients into the cell.

The membrane also holds in the **cytoplasm**. The cytoplasm has the texture of jelly. It holds the organelles inside the cell in place. The cytoplasm takes up most of the space inside a cell. Think of a cell as fruit in a gelatin salad. The cytoplasm is the gelatin, and the fruit are the organelles. The membrane is the container that holds the cell together, just as a bowl holds the salad.

The blood cells of a frog look like a river of frog eyes.

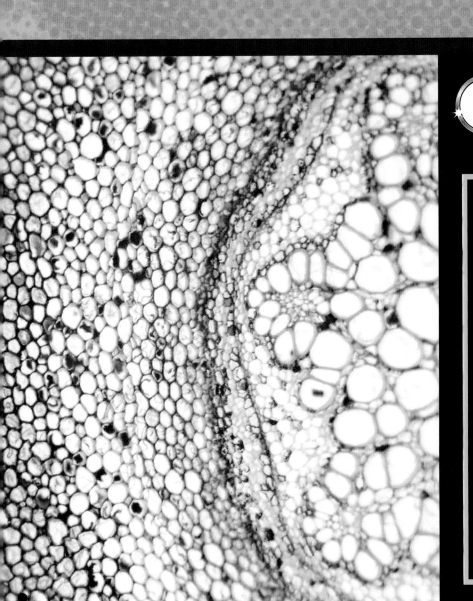

The Complexities of Life
Animals are, in many ways, more complex organisms than plants. However, plant cells are more complex than animal cells. Plants produce their own foods. Plants must withstand forces from nature without protective coverings. They must survive without shelter. Plants also have more kinds of cell structures than animal cells do.

A cross section of a rotting fern shows the plant's complexity.

Plant and animal cells also have **mitochondria**. These organelles take nutrients from the cell and turn them into energy. A cell that needs a lot of energy can have thousands of mitochondria. Cells that need less energy need far fewer of these organelles. If a cell needs more energy, it can make more mitochondria.

17

Root, Stem, Leaf

Nearly every plant has three basic types of cells: cells in the leaves, cells in the stems, and cells in the roots. Each type of cell has a different job.

Because of their different jobs, the cells look and behave in distinct ways. Let's start at the bottom. Roots absorb water and minerals. So cells in the roots must be able to move water and minerals. These cells tend to be narrow, long, and hollow. The walls of these cells are strong. Their structure allows **water-transport cells** to keep their shape as they absorb and release water, instead of bursting or collapsing. You can find water-transport cells in stems, branches, and trunks, too.

Other cells look similar to water-transport cells. The **sieve tube cells** move sugars to the parts of the plant that need food. Fruit, flowers, and roots cannot make food. The sieve tube cells move food from the leaves to the other parts.

Other cells support plants and allow them to stand up. One type of support cell is found at the places where the plant grows. These **support cells** are flexible. This allows the plant to stretch and move as it grows. The other support cells are in older, firmer parts of the plant. These support cells are very strong, which is what gives wood its hardness.

The older parts of a plant have cells that are firm. The new growth has cells that are structured to be more flexible.

The roots have special cells both to move water and to move sugars.

Leaves are full of ordinary plant cells that store food and water and give off sugar.

Most of the rest of the cells in plants are known as typical plant cells. They store energy. They take in water and nutrients. They give off extra sugars that can travel to other cells. These ordinary cells make up most of a plant.

giant redwood trees

Cells in Common
Most plants have the same types of cells. The tiny amazing duckweed plant has leaves, stems, a root, and flowers. This means that it has water-transport cells, sieve tube cells, support cells, and "typical" cells. In this way, tiny duckweed is like the huge plant known as the giant redwood.

19

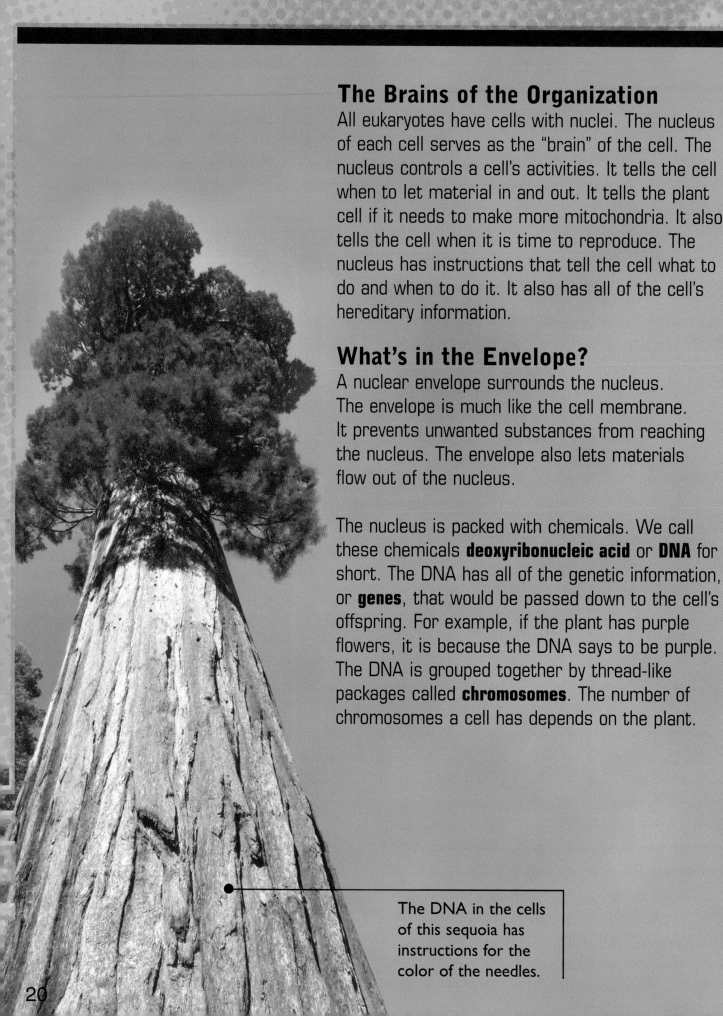

The Brains of the Organization

All eukaryotes have cells with nuclei. The nucleus of each cell serves as the "brain" of the cell. The nucleus controls a cell's activities. It tells the cell when to let material in and out. It tells the plant cell if it needs to make more mitochondria. It also tells the cell when it is time to reproduce. The nucleus has instructions that tell the cell what to do and when to do it. It also has all of the cell's hereditary information.

What's in the Envelope?

A nuclear envelope surrounds the nucleus. The envelope is much like the cell membrane. It prevents unwanted substances from reaching the nucleus. The envelope also lets materials flow out of the nucleus.

The nucleus is packed with chemicals. We call these chemicals **deoxyribonucleic acid** or **DNA** for short. The DNA has all of the genetic information, or **genes**, that would be passed down to the cell's offspring. For example, if the plant has purple flowers, it is because the DNA says to be purple. The DNA is grouped together by thread-like packages called **chromosomes**. The number of chromosomes a cell has depends on the plant.

The DNA in the cells of this sequoia has instructions for the color of the needles.

Chromosomes are wound a bit like a chain of chromosome pairs. When a cell nucleus gives instructions to reproduce, the chromosomes inside it line up. The cell, including the nucleus, splits. The chain breaks apart, so one strand of chromosome goes to each part of the split cell.

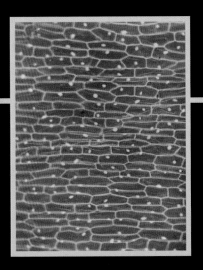

In the Middle!
If you look at a cell under a microscope, the nucleus should be somewhere in the middle of the cell. It floats in the cytoplasm. The nucleus will never be at the edge of the cell. That positioning protects the nucleus when something bumps the cell.

DNA is arranged in a double helix. It looks like a twisted ladder, as this model shows.

Going Green

Plants are able to produce their own food. Plants do not depend on anything but sunlight and water for survival. Humans or other animals cannot do that. Animals need plants or other animals to survive.

leaf

Energy from the Sun powers everything on Earth. The heat and light energy changes to energy that plants and animals can use. For plants, this process, called **photosynthesis**, takes place inside the leaves. During photosynthesis, the plant takes in water from the roots, carbon dioxide from the air, and light from the Sun. The plant performs a chemical reaction. It makes oxygen and sugar. The sugar feeds the plant, as well as anything that eats the plant.

The cells that perform photosynthesis are in the middle of the leaf. You can tell these cells from others because they contain organelles called **chloroplasts**.

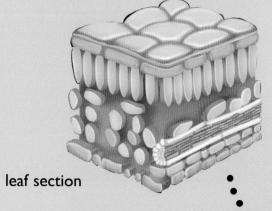

leaf section

One cell will have many chloroplasts. The cells that perform photosynthesis give plants their green color. If a part of a plant is not green, there are no energy-producing cells in that part. Picture roots you have seen. Roots are not green. So you know no photosynthesis happens in the roots.

mesophyll cell

Chloroplasts are interesting organelles. They make the food that feeds the plant. Chloroplasts have DNA inside. If more chloroplasts are needed, they can reproduce without waiting for the nucleus to divide.

A main part of the chloroplast is the **granum**. Stacked together, many granums make grana. One chloroplast contains stacks and stacks of grana, where carbon dioxide (the air we breathe out) reacts with water and sunlight. The grana create sugar and oxygen. The sugar and oxygen are released from the grana, from the chloroplasts, and from the cell. This process happens all day long.

granum

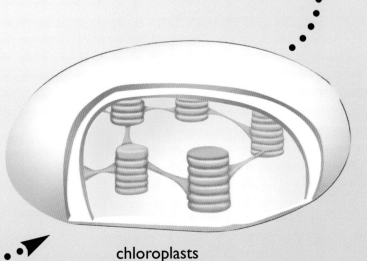

chloroplasts

Color Me Green
Most tree leaves have yellow and orange coloring, not just green. For most of the year, **chlorophyll** covers up the yellow and orange coloring. In autumn, trees produce less chlorophyll. This lets the other colors show through. This is how leaves change color with the seasons. The red and purple pigments, or coloring, are not usually in most green leaves. These pigments form in cool night temperatures.

Plant Food per bag – N 10.0 kg P₂O₅ 4.0 kg K₂O 7.0 kg

EEC FERTILIZER

NPK FERTILIZER	20 . 8 . 14
TOTAL Nitrogen (N)	20.0%
Ammoniacal Nitrogen	11.0%
Nitric Nitrogen	9.0%
Phosphorus Pentoxide (P₂O₅)	
Soluble in Neutral Ammonium Citrate + Water	8.0% (3.5%P)
Soluble in Water	7.2% (3.1%P)
Potassium Oxide (K₂O)	
Soluble in Water	14.0% (11.6%K)

Weight 50 kg 110 lb net

ICI Fertilisers P.O. Box 1, Billingham, Cleveland TS23 1LB

STORE UNDER COVER.   OUTDOOR STACKS MUST BE SHEETED SECURELY.

Great Chemistry

Plants depend on many chemicals to grow and reproduce. Some plant cells create a chemical reaction using heat, carbon dioxide, and water. How? Carbon dioxide is made of **molecules** of carbon and oxygen. Water is made of molecules of hydrogen and oxygen. The chemicals hydrogen, oxygen, and carbon change forms. They become sugar and pure oxygen.

The NPK values on a bag of fertilizer show the amounts of nitrogen, phosphorous, and potassium the fertilizer contains.

Sugar is made of the chemicals carbon, hydrogen, and oxygen. The plants strip the carbon from carbon dioxide and the hydrogen from water. Some of the oxygen needed to make sugar comes from water.

Plants also need the chemical nitrogen. Plants use nitrogen as they grow. Without enough nitrogen, a plant may be pale green or yellow. The cells are not able to reproduce without it, so growth slows down or even stops.

Phosphorous comes into use when a plant produces flowers, fruits, and seeds. Plants that get enough phosphorous have stronger stems and branches. If a plant does not get enough phosphorous, it may not grow to its full size. It also may not be able to defend itself from diseases. Potassium protects plants from stresses. Plants can absorb too much salt or other minerals when the land where they are growing is flooded. Potassium helps the plant protect itself from harm when this happens. In addition, potassium helps support the cells that transport water and food through the plant.

Where does a plant get these and other important chemicals? Some come from the soil. Healthy soil has many of these chemicals. Some soils have too little of one or more nutrients. In these cases, plant foods and fertilizers can provide the missing chemicals.

In the Lab

Green Medicine

Many modern medicines use the chemicals in plants. The heart medicine digitalis comes from the foxglove flower. Doctors can treat childhood cancer with chemicals in the Madagascar vinca. Both foxglove and vinca can grow in a home garden.

Trapped! Meat-Eating Plants

Plants must have nitrogen to grow and survive. For plants growing in healthy soil, getting nitrogen is not a problem. However, some plants grow in poor soil, and some grow in nearly no soil. Their survival depends on genetic **adaptations**.

Many of these plants are **carnivorous**. This means they consume animals for nutrients. They absorb nitrogen from the bodies of animals. Carnivorous plants have traps to catch insects, frogs, worms, and even small mammals.

One type of trap is called a pitfall, or pitcher. A pitcher often has a colorful lip that attracts insects. The plant makes a slick coating around insects it traps, to keep them from climbing out. Then the plant produces a liquid that drowns the insect and dissolves the body. Some plants have lids on their pitchers to keep out rainwater.

The carnivorous plant is beautiful to attract prey.

Some traps snap shut. When an insect lands on the leaves of a snapping trap, the leaves close up. The insect wiggles and fights, which is a cue for the leaves to grow together. The leaves form a kind of stomach around the prey. Then the plant makes a substance that digests the insect.

Yet others have a pouch, or bladder, with a small opening and a couple of hairs. When a baby mosquito, a tadpole, or a bug touches the hairs, the opening widens. The bladder sucks the prey in. Then the trap shuts and digests the prey. This type of plant can continue to trap insects while it digests meals.

Shut Your Trap
The trap of an Asian pitcher plant (shown far left) can hold over two gallons (7.6 liters) of liquid. Thirsty birds, lizards, mice, and other animals are tempted to drink from the trap. When this happens, the pitcher plant gets a huge meal and a large dose of nitrogen!

The Venus flytrap has sticky leaves that can hold an insect while its leaves close around it.

Fern Family

Cells reproduce so a plant can grow larger. Entire plants reproduce so new plants can grow. Some plants depend on sexual reproduction. This means that there are male and female cells that combine to make a new plant.

Ferns, for example, create **spores** to make new ferns. A grown fern plant makes a spore case. The case may be under a leaf or on a stem or leaf of its own. When the spores are ready, the case breaks open, and the wind carries the spores away. If the spores land somewhere warm, dark, and moist, they can begin to reproduce.

To reproduce, the spore grows tiny roots to hold it in place. Then it makes male and female plant parts. These two parts create the cells that produce a new fern. The male and female cells each have their own DNA. These two sets of DNA combine to make a new plant.

Fern Reproduction

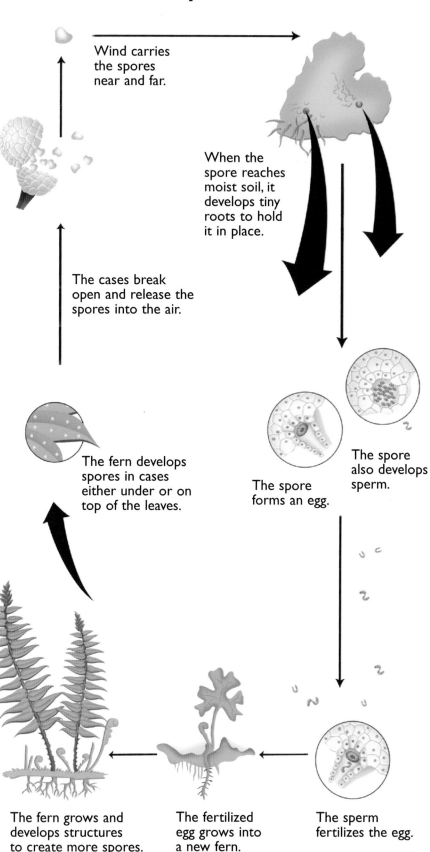

Wind carries the spores near and far.

When the spore reaches moist soil, it develops tiny roots to hold it in place.

The cases break open and release the spores into the air.

The fern develops spores in cases either under or on top of the leaves.

The spore forms an egg.

The spore also develops sperm.

The fern grows and develops structures to create more spores.

The fertilized egg grows into a new fern.

The sperm fertilizes the egg.

A fern can make its own male and female cells. Or a male cell from one fern can fertilize a female cell from another fern. The female cell is an egg. As soon as the egg is fertilized, it grows a root and a stem. Once this tiny new fern can grow leaves, the plant can feed itself. The fern grows. It creates new spore cases and starts the process all over again.

This Japanese painted fern is one of thousands of plants that reproduce by making spores.

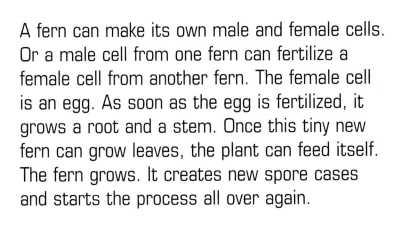

In the Lab

Fossil Record

Fossils show that ferns used to produce seeds instead of spores. Ferns were at one time the most common type of plant on Earth. Oil and other fossil fuels are made up of decomposed ferns that once grew as tall as trees.

Going to Seed

Spores are not **seeds**. Most plants that people have in their yards, gardens, and farms reproduce by seed. Plants that produce seeds have offspring from yet another kind of sexual reproduction.

Seed-bearing plants make flowers. The flowers on a plant have male parts, female parts, or both. In some plants, the flower can fertilize itself. In other plants, a different flower, often from a completely different plant, must fertilize a female flower.

Male flowers produce **pollen**. The pollen is what makes allergy-sufferers sneeze. Pollen can travel on the wind. A bee can carry pollen on its body. You can be a carrier as well if pollen brushes on your clothes or some other part of you. When the pollen reaches a female flower, it travels down a tube. At the bottom of the tube is the female cell or egg. The pollen fertilizes the egg, and the seed begins to form.

Seed Reproduction

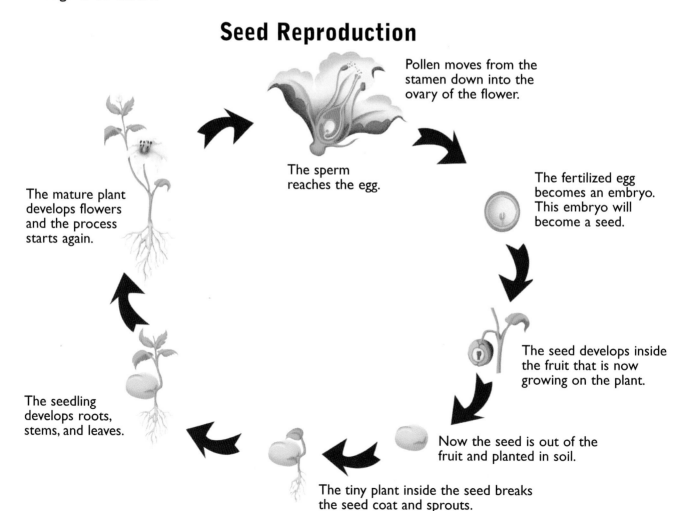

Pollen moves from the stamen down into the ovary of the flower.

The sperm reaches the egg.

The fertilized egg becomes an embryo. This embryo will become a seed.

The seed develops inside the fruit that is now growing on the plant.

Now the seed is out of the fruit and planted in soil.

The tiny plant inside the seed breaks the seed coat and sprouts.

The seedling develops roots, stems, and leaves.

The mature plant develops flowers and the process starts again.

Parts of a Seed

The seed that forms has a tiny plant inside. This plant is what sprouts when the seed has been planted. Along with the plant is at least one **cotyledon**. The seed will either have one or two cotyledons, which are like leaves. The cotyledon contains food to keep the tiny plant alive until it can produce leaves and roots to get its own food and nutrients.

This female blossom has a tiny squash behind it.

On the Wind

Conifers are evergreen plants that produce cones. These plants have male and female cones instead of flowers. Since the female cones are difficult to pollinate, the male cones produce tremendous amounts of pollen. When the pollen is ready, the male cone opens enough so that the wind flows into it. The cone releases pollen that can blow into a female cone.

One for All

Not every plant produces seeds or spores. Some plants do not use male and female cells to make new plants. Plants that reproduce sexually have offspring that are different from the parent plants. The offspring have different genes. The offspring plants of plants that reproduce asexually are identical to the parents.

Asexual reproduction works in many ways. Sometimes new plants can come from **cuttings**. A gardener may take a cutting of a plant and put it in water or soil. The cut part of the plant can start forming roots. When the roots have grown enough, the cutting can be planted.

The spider plant reproduces by **division**. It makes small plants along its stem.

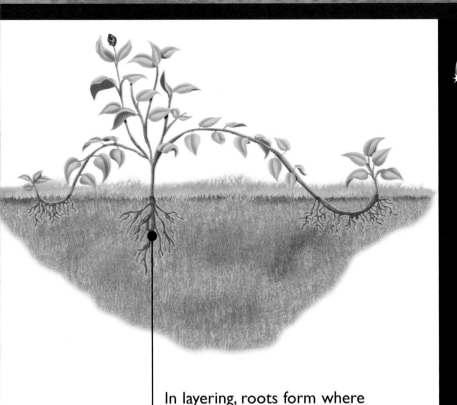

In layering, roots form where a plant and soil touch.

Roots of the Problem

Have you ever pulled a weed, only to have the same weed grow back in the same place? It came back because the plant was able to reproduce from root cells left behind. Cutting was the process at work. The root left behind broke off from the main plant.

Many plants are able to make offspring on their own. A stem or branch of a plant touches the ground. The cells of the plant sense that they are touching soil. The plant creates roots at the point where the plant and the soil are in contact. When the roots take hold, the little plant can be cut away from the parent plant. This process is known as **layering**.

You may not notice that a plant has produced offspring until you dig up the plant. Some plants develop small plants that grow right along with the parent. For example, a spider plant sends out stems with "pups" growing on them. The spider plant reproduces by a process called division. The pup can be cut off and planted.

A cutting can be as small as a few cells.

Tubers and Rhizomes and Corms! Oh, My!

Layering, cutting, and division are not the only ways that plants reproduce without seeds or spores. Some plants have special underground structures that allow them to create offspring. Two plants can also combine in ways that do not involve male and female cells.

Many plants store food in swollen stems or other structures in the ground. These structures are bulbs, tubers, corms, and rhizomes. Differences among the four have to do with how they grow. The four structures are more alike than different. The plants that have these structures include potatoes, onions, and yams. These plant parts feed the plant when the plant cannot make enough of its own food.

Bulbs, tubers, corms, and rhizomes can all make new plants. If you keep a potato around too long, you can see it happen. The tuber sprouts "eyes." You can remove the eye along with a chunk of potato, plant it, and it will grow. Nearly all plants that store food underground can reproduce from their underground storage units.

All of the cloves in this head of garlic could be planted to start new, identical garlic plants.

Each eye on this tuber is the start of a new plant.

Dandelion DNA helps the plants survive despite being run over by mowers.

Grafting

For many types of fruit trees, the best way to make new plants is by **grafting**. To graft trees, a branch of one type of tree is placed into a cut in another type of tree. Eventually, the cut tree grows around the grafted branch. The grafted branch grows normally.

Why use grafting? Some plants make great fruits, but weak wood. If a branch of great fruit can grow on a tree with strong wood, then the fruit can grow freely on a tree that will not break as easily.

Flowers on the Lawn
Some dandelions propagate asexually with seeds. The seeds form with no pollen and with just one plant. Like grafted fruits or potatoes with eyes, the new dandelion is identical to its parent.

Chapter 4

Related Research

For thousands of years, farmers have improved their crops. Because of selective breeding, wheat and other crops grow more quickly, resist diseases, and are more nutritious. Yet the price for these improvements may be high.

Growing plants with desirable traits is the basis of agriculture. Let's say you have two varieties of corn. One variety grows quickly. The other variety resists numerous diseases. You can try combining these desirable traits into a new corn variety.

Corn seeds are kept safe in vaults throughout the world.

Selective breeding has greatly improved the world's food production, especially in the last 60 years. Crops are more disease-resistant. Some crops produce a harvest twice in the same year.

Picking and choosing traits might sound like the solution for world hunger. But selective breeding has a downside. Modern varieties of major crops, such as wheat, are genetically similar to one another. When selective breeding creates a new species of that crop, the genetic differences are fewer. This can leave the crop more vulnerable to illness. An epidemic happens when a large percentage of the world's crops are infected.

Scientists have a plan to try to encourage genetic diversity. They have created a bank that stores genetically diverse crop varieties. These crop varieties still have "wild" strains of genetic material in them. In the future, these stored genes may create new species of crops.

In the Lab

Like Money in the Bank
The Svalbard Global Seed Vault is on an island in the Arctic Circle. The vault plays a vital role for humanity. It holds spare seeds from around the world and keeps the seeds frozen. If a large-scale disaster wiped out seed banks in a particular region, the seeds in the vault could help people recover a new supply.

Svalbard Global Seed Vault

Book 'Em!

We all have fingerprints. Our prints are one way that each of us can be identified. In a similar way, DNA can identify plant species. Plants also have prints that are all their own.

Plant fingerprinting begins with mapping the DNA of a species. Like humans, a plant species has unique DNA. When researchers look at the DNA of plants within the same species, however, the researchers have to look even closer.

All roses are in the same plant species. Yet there are thousands of rose varieties called cultivars. Each cultivar has unique traits such as color, petal size, or height. At the DNA level, these differences show up as **molecular markers**.

These DNA markers can be difficult to detect, so advanced technologies are needed. Using heating and cooling techniques and special equipment, the DNA strands are carefully broken apart. This allows the researchers to separate key portions of the DNA for study.

After thoroughly examining the DNA, scientists create a profile for the plant cultivar. This profile becomes the cultivar's fingerprint. Many companies make money using plant cultivars they have created, so this information is useful to businesses. Sometimes companies have to prove their ownership of a cultivar.

Your fingerprints are all your own. The same is true of plants and their molecular markers.

Your Very Own Species
It is possible for someone to own a plant species. A researcher can take out a patent on a cultivar he or she created. A patent is a legal way to claim that you invented something unique. Using this patent, the inventor can make a lot of money from his or her invention.

DNA fingerprinting is incredibly important in medical research. Scientists have created many medical products from plants. Sometimes, plants that are similar to each other can be confused. Fingerprinting these plants can ensure that the right plant is used in the medicine.

This Muskogee crepe myrtle is a unique cultivar in its species.

Chapter 5

Future Growth

You see custom-made products every day. Cars and clothing are just some of the things made with specific features. The same customization now works for plants.

Genetic engineering is a direct method of changing DNA in living things. A scientist cuts away a desirable part of a plant's DNA and places that trait into another plant's DNA. With the right equipment, a researcher can determine exactly where to make the cut.

A DNA strand breaks into small parts called **sequences.** For example, a plant's disease resistance is in a specific sequence. Through careful experiments, researchers can break the code and determine the specific sequences.

A large portion of the cotton grown in the United Kingdom has been modified to resist pests.

Brazilian farmers have been planting genetically modified soybeans.

Gold Standard
One challenge for solving world food shortages is growing food packed with nutrition. Rice is crucial to the diet of millions of people, but it often lacks vitamin A. Researchers successfully added genetic material from daffodils and bacteria to help golden rice produce the missing vitamin.

The most common form of genetic engineering is molecular **cloning**. First, a scientist removes the desired segment from the DNA. Then, the scientist attaches the segment to a living DNA in bacteria. Researchers use bacteria partly because the tiny organisms grow and reproduce very quickly. Many copies, or clones, of the DNA segment form this way. Finally, the scientist removes the segments and adds them to the original plant species.

One of the most useful applications of genetic engineering has been for increasing food production. Insect and disease resistance are important for crop success. Researchers have genetically modified numerous crops, including soybeans and corn, for these traits. Genetic engineering will be crucial in meeting the world's food production needs.

Seeds of Controversy

Changing plants on the cellular level has created a revolution in food production and a wider variety of beautiful garden plants. It has also created a lot of controversy. Are modified foods safe to eat? Who owns the seeds of custom-made flowers and crops?

Many companies are in the business of creating engineered crops. Their research and development have helped feed millions of people in poor countries. Sometimes, the genes of these modified seeds get into the DNA of normal crops. When that happens, a company and farmers might find themselves in court, arguing over who owns the newly modified crops.

From the beginning, people have suspected genetically modified foods of being unhealthy, and even dangerous. Governments and universities have studied this issue closely for many years. So far, researchers have found that most modified foods are just as healthful as normal foods. Health concerns linger, however. Pollen from modified corn is known to hurt butterflies. Some researchers think that people will develop new allergies.

DNA of Arctic cod was used to make some plants cold-hardy.

Research on plant cells continues to turn out amazing products. A potential source of energy is from renewable plant parts called **biomass**. Researchers can genetically modify plants to create biomass that can turn into biofuel.

Another exciting area for development is in medicine. In the last twenty years, researchers have used genetic engineering to treat some diseases. In addition, doctors use gene therapy to treat medical conditions of babies who are still in the womb. The potential benefits of genetic engineering appear to be endless. How, do you think, should we control it all?

A community depends on farmers growing safe and healthy crops.

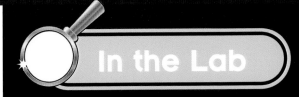

New Money
Societies rise and fall on their ability to produce food for people. To protect against crop diseases and other disasters, we must be certain that we use a wide variety of seeds and plants. Seeds are more valuable than gold!

43

Notebook

Science Fair

Use a common plant to test its ability to reproduce.

Materials:

- Geranium plant
- 3 pint-sized clear jars
- Paper clips
- Distilled water
- Dental floss
- 3 drinking straws
- Liquid root stimulator (optional)

Method:

1. Fill each jar 2/3 full with distilled water.
2. If using root stimulator, add the correct amount to the water, based on the instructions.
3. Cut one portion of a leaf, one stem with leaves, and one clump of roots from the plant.
4. Cut a 10-inch (25-cm) length of dental floss.
5. Tie one end of the floss to the middle of the straw. Tie the other end to the paper clip.
6. Attach a plant cutting to each of the three paper clips.
7. Lay the straw across the top of the jar. Hang the plant cutting and paper clip so that the cutting is partly under water. The cut portion should be in the water.
8. Set the jars in a sunny window for two weeks. Keep the water level constant. Observe which cuttings develop new roots, stems, or leaves.

For Further Information

Books

Johnson, Rebecca L. **Microquests: Powerful Plant Cells.**
Minneapolis: Millbrook Press, 2007.

Stephens, Nicholas. **Green World: Plant Cells and Tissues.**
New York: Chelsea House Publications, 2006.

Stille, Darlene P. **Exploring Science—Plant Cells: The Building
Blocks of Plants.** Minneapolis: Compass Point Books, 2006.

Web sites

www.plantcell.org

www.biology4kids.com

urbanext.illinois.edu/gpe/

Until man duplicates a blade of grass,
nature can laugh at his so-called
scientific knowledge. . . . It's obvious
that we don't know one millionth
of one percent about anything.

Thomas Alva Edison

Glossary

adaptations Characteristics that are favorable for organisms over time

allele Gene that determines a genetic trait

binomial nomenclature Method of naming plants with two words, the genus and the species, in Latin

biomass Plant material or waste used as energy source

botany The study of plant life

carnivorous Eats meat

cells Smallest units that make up every living thing

chlorophyll Green pigments in organisms capable of photosynthesis

chloroplasts The organelles that contain chlorophyll and perform photosynthesis

chromosomes Coiled threads of DNA containing genes

cloning Creating a genetically identical organism

cotyledon Leaf in the embryo of a plant that grows from a seed

cultivars Plants created on purpose

cutting Way of creating a plant from pieces of another plant

cytoplasm The jelly-like material in the cell outside of the nucleus

deoxyribonucleic acid (DNA) Long strand of genetic information found in the cell's nucleus

division Way to make new plants by dividing root material

dominant The trait that will show itself even if it is on only one chromosome

eukaryotes Organisms made of cells that have a nucleus

genes Sections of a chromosome that code for a certain protein

genus A major ranking of organisms

grafting Way to make new plants by joining cuts of plants

granum A stack of plant materials that contain chlorophyll

hybrid Offspring of two parents with different traits

layering Way to make new plants when parts of certain plants meet soil

mitochondria Part of the cell that converts nutrients into energy

molecular markers Sequences of DNA that are known

molecules Groups of atoms

nucleus Control center of a plant or animal cell

organelles General name for parts of a cell

photosynthesis The process of making food from water, carbon dioxide, and light

plasma membranes Organelles that allow material to pass in and out of cells

pollen Plant powder that contains the male cells that form seed plants

recessive The trait that will show itself if the code for it is on both chromosomes

seeds Plants in the embryonic stage

selective breeding Choosing plants or animals to breed based on their characteristics

sequences In genetics, lines of letters representing chemical structure

sieve tube cells The cells in the tissues of the plant that move sugars

species A classification of like organisms, more specific than a genus

spores Reproductive cells in mold and fungi and plants that do not flower

support cells Plants that support an organism against gravity and like forces

water-transport cells Cells in stems, branches, trunks, and roots that help move water through the plant

Index